Peeling the Onion
Poems of Spiritual Awakening

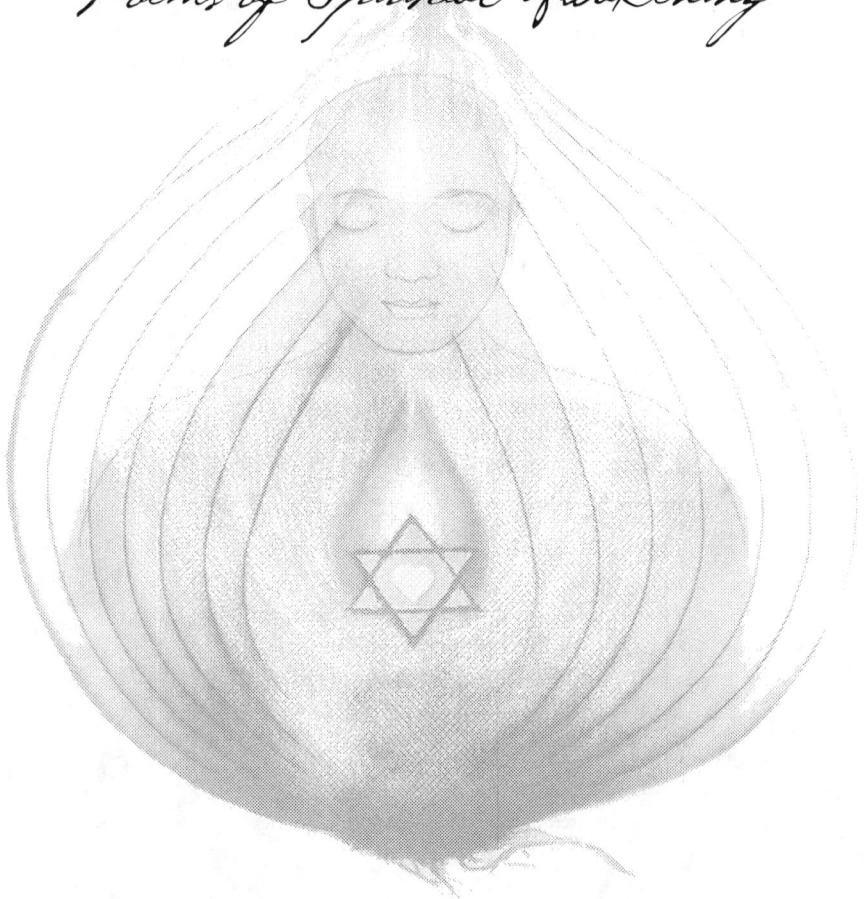

George E. James, M.S.

PUBLISHED BY: First World Publishing

James, George E., 1948-

Peeling the Onion: Poems of Spiritual Awakening

George E. James—1st edition.

ISBN: 978-1-59540-893-8 Paperback
ISBN: 978-1-59540-894-5 Hardcover
ISBN: 978-1-59540-895-2 ebook
Library of Congress Catalog Number: 2006937250

EDITED BY: Diane Frank

BOOK COVER ILLUSTRATION BY Seth K. Hughes and Mille Odgen
PHOTO CREDIT: Tom Kochel
GRAPHIC DESIGN: Sandy Hughes

Printed in the United States of America

Foreword

This is a brilliant and beautiful book. George James' poetic narrative reflects the gradual unfolding of the experience of his own primordial and innate awareness field becoming experientially visible and available. Both the luminosity of his experience and the difficulties of his innermost life blend in a manner which is both completely authentic and completely uplifting. This book will be most useful to people of faith and to people of no faith, uplifting to readers who have a strong interest in contemporary spirituality and to those who have no interest whatsoever in the embodiment of Divinity. This is a good story and everyone who reads it will be drawn in and become absorbed in this most human drama. This book reflects with clarity the timeless quest for consciousness.

RUDOLPH BAUER, Ph.D.
Diplomate in Clinical Psychology
American Board of Professional Psychology

Co-Director The Washington Center for Consciousness Studies
Washington,D.C.

Contents

chapter one
AWAKENED TO SLEEP

chapter two
LIVING DEAD

chapter three
WHISPERED AWAKE

chapter four
EXPLORING AND HEALING MYSELF

chapter five
SOUL REVIVAL

INVITATION

Gratitude

Now that I have been through the experience of co-authoring a book, my naïveté about how hard could it be to write a book has been completely wiped out. My experience has allowed me to appreciate and relate more personally to all those introductions and dedications to loved ones for putting up with the author and their writing process.

I extend a great big hug of gratitude first to my friend and editor, Diane Frank, for opening me up to the conscious poet who was suffering in the closet. Your loving skill, guidance, and intellectual challenge helped to move this book from seven years of frustration to a book in print.

To my Eastern spiritual teacher, Maharishi Mahesh Yogi, I offer my deepest heartfelt thanks for reawakening the transcendental state of consciousness in me. To Sri Ravi Shankar, I offer my deepest heartfelt thanks for rekindling and deepening my awareness of the power of God's breath in me and for helping me to further deepen my consciousness and gifts from the Divine. God bless you both for making yourselves available to me, so that I could learn and experience how to open up my mind to another way. In the tradition of the East, I offer you my pranam. Yes, in spite of my emotional as well as physical unstressing and my western way of telling you like it is, during the learning process, I did have a measure of fun.

To my first healing teachers, Shirley Hortsman, Ethel Lombardi, and Ernestine Mitchner, who were on the cutting edge long before it was chic and required a Ph.D., thank you for sharing your gifts with the World. To Connie Newton, founder of Integrated Awareness Technique©, and The Perceptive Awareness Training Institute©, the refiner, polisher and expander of my intuition and healing capabilities, thank you and your absolutely fabulous husband Jim for being such wonderful western role models and inspirations for service to humanity. And to my many friends, visible and invisible, I thank you for your love, support and encouragement.

To my friends, Wes Dias, Bethany O'Halloran, Michael Spitzer, and Ann Wutchiett, who proofed my many drafts and rewrites, thank you for your love, friendship and encouragement. To my friend Sylvia Somerville, whose initial edit of my writing helped me to put my voice into my writing process, your loving, poignant yet gentle criticisms, suggestions, encouragement, and guidance during my writing process were a blessing to me. Thank you for finding and taking time from your busy schedule and family responsibilities. I love you and send you and your family many blessings.

To Susan Chernak McElroy, thank you for sharing your professional writer's expertise, insights, criticism and experience. Although I was wet behind the ears, your words helped me to let go and take the deeper step into objectivity to help refine my voice as a writer.

To Ms. Vickie, thank you and a great big hug for your support in the final birthing of this book.

To my humble and generous friend —you know who you are— who extended friendship, kindness, generosity and laughter, and who graciously opened your home to me during a very difficult phase of my growth process, you asked me not to acknowledge you for your acts, for that is your humble nature. My mind wanted to comply with your request; however, my heart was and still is so full of gratitude that I could not contain nor silence its voice, so forgive me as I honor you in this small way.

To my spiritual midwives, goddesses, and healing colleagues, Erica Lazaro, my friend and acupuncturist, and Dr. D. Shinkle, my chiropractor; thank you and God bless you for your patient and technical skills in helping me give birth to my new body-mind-Soul connection.

To spiritual brothers, Rudy Bauer, Ph.D. and Bill Bauman, Ph.D., your intellect and skill helped me gain an understanding which was a tremendous blessing for me as my world turned inside out and upside down as I stepped through my crack in the Cosmic Egg.

To my wonderful clients, who have provided me with the opportunity to contribute my gifts to their journey, thank you for giving me the opportunity to serve you in God's name. It has been a great joy to watch you unfold on your journey. And to the many people who entered and exited my life to contribute to my growth, thank you and may God's blessing be with you as you walk your path on your journey home.

And to you my dear reader, regardless of whether you're a novice or deep in the trenches of your journey, I thank you for choosing my book to be a part of your journey of Self-discovery.

In love forever,
George James

Prologue

"Each individual has to take responsibility for the lessons they've received and weave them into his or her understanding of their purpose."

(GEJ/SOUL 10/13/96)

In this world there are people whose sole desire is to have their words read by others for fame and glory. This is not my goal, for I know that fame or glory is only temporary. My goal is to be within my source of creation 24 hours a day non-stop, however, I forgot to check the Divine Plan.

Unlike most seventeen year olds my worry was not about college but how I was going to survive life once I left the children's home I lived in for seven years.

One day, in English class, a strange phenomenon started happening to me and continued throughout my life. Filled with self-judgment, confusion, fear and embarrassment, I hid the results of my strange phenomenon from my closest friends and I never revealed it to any of my lovers.

On August 5, 1982 during meditation I had an experience where I felt my sternum split in half and my chest was opened like a book. I was so overwhelmed with emotions I started to cry. As I cried I felt and saw a white light flow down into my head and out through my exposed heart. This experience lasted for 2 hours. When it ended I thought my psychological world was crumbling and I was loosing touch with reality. To touch base and get a reality check I called the mother of my friend Kim, Donee Casper, who was a psychotherapist in Seattle. As I was about to hang-up the phone to prepare for my appointment she said, "Bring your poetry journal with you."

Her comment surprised and shocked me since not even my closest friends knew I had been secretly writing since my senior year in high school. During my session with Donee she encouraged me to share what I had written with others, but I declined because I felt "no they're just me, nothing anyone I didn't know could use." After our session as I was preparing to leave she looked at me and said: "Send me a copy to read." I attempted to pull it together for her, however, I never made it. Inside I wasn't ready to be that exposed and vulnerable to anyone, including those who loved me.

So how and why am I now sharing my poetic reflection of my spiritual journey?

In 1988, after a special intuition course I had taken, I began the routine of having a conscious, interactive dialog with my Soul. After meditating I would ask my Soul for either clarification of some event, topic, etc., or a question that was on my mind then I would write it in my journal. Throughout the entire month of December 1991, during meditation, I kept seeing vivid scenarios of myself writing a book and having a fireside chat with Oprah Winfrey. I found these thoughts to be distracting since I didn't consider myself to be a writer, and I had only seen a video clip of Oprah once. After a month of being annoyed by these ridiculous visions and thoughts I decided to ask my Soul to clarify the purpose of these thoughts. So on December 31, 1991, I asked, "Are these scenarios of me writing a book purposeful, or am I releasing some unresolved stress in my system?" My Soul's response was:

> "It is both and more, for it is serving to help you open and clarify your pathway. The observer nature of Self is of utmost importance to the process of higher consciousness. This point has been reiterated over and over to you, Beloved. Now that you have a clearer grasp of the process, just allow the process to move you, and surely your heart will open even more to receive."

> "The sensitivity of your feeling is important, for you have understood correctly Jesus' lesson, 'Unless ye become like little children: vulnerable, open, in the present, quick to forgive, always ready to Love.' These are children's qualities that you, Beloved, are cultivating and nurturing; and the fruits will appear. Amen."

I wrote the message down, read it and put it away. I figured if I didn't dwell on it, it would go away. However, over the next six years, from time to time, I would receive gentle nudges from my Soul to pursue the idea, or vision of writing a book. Rather than follow through on them, I tried to weasel my way out of it with all sorts of excuses. I rationalized these nudges as "stress release," and went on with my life for about seven years. No matter how reticent I was, my Soul's love and gentle persistence finally won out and I surrendered to the task in 1997.

My next "book nudge" came in the spring of 1997. However, this time the "nudge" moved into reality. I was in Brooklyn, New York seeing clients at the home of my spiritual sister Clair, and her family. After my morning meditation, as I was sitting quietly, my Soul started our dialog with a series of questions to me that went like this:

SOUL: *"What did God ask King Solomon?"*

ME: "God asked King Solomon what power he wanted from Him."

SOUL: *"What was Solomon's request?"*

ME: "Solomon asked God for 'Understanding.'"

SOUL: *"How did God respond to this?"*

ME: "God recognized that King Solomon was very wise and trust-worthy, so he gave him understanding and more."

SOUL: *"Now, Beloved One, as you strive to piece together your journey, to help you focus we suggest that you consider the main purpose of the task to be 'to get ye Understanding.' For when you understand the journey, you come into the power of God's Plan!"*

The first task that had to be accomplished was to gather my earthly experiences together into a cohesive manner, so that the Soul could do its job. What followed was my mind being flooded with many ideas and thoughts for a book. I began to write frantically in my attempt to get everything down that came into my head.

After the initial book download, I became comfortable with receiving information for the book, and one morning, a few weeks into the process, my Soul felt I was ready to receive another part of the book's title. During my dialog with my Soul, I heard the words, *"A Soul's point of view of a modern mystic's journey."* I asked: "What does this mean?" My Soul suggested that that sentence be included in the book's title. My first response was: "No way!" I told my Soul that the sentence contained loaded words that would trigger many preconceived concepts: And that this would generate negative feedback from people, and I didn't want that to happen. Needless to say, that argument meant absolutely nothing to my Soul.

I was not a happy camper about this and one day during my dialog with my Soul about the book, it made it clear to my conscious mind that this book is not "George's explanation of the journey." This book is about my Soul's explanation of the understanding *it* has come to know from "*its*" journey through George, its manifest expression. And, to celebrate the realization of "*its*" journey here on earth. This manifestation known as George, from the Soul's point of view, is just another garment worn on this journey that didn't have to first be dissolved in order to "*get ye understanding.*"

My friend, you would think after the above realization that I would have fully acquiesced to the process. Nope! Read on.

While engaged in my morning meditation, the Saturday after Christmas of 1997, I became aware that at the level of my subconscious mind, I still had questions and concerns about the title given for this book.

As I continued to settle deeper into that quiet, all-knowing space in time, another insight was revealed about the mechanics and effects of the title, to help answer my subconscious inquiry.

What I discovered was that each word the Soul had chosen, "*Get Ye Understanding: A Soul's Point of View of a Modern Mystic's Journey,*" was filled with profound insight. I was so excited by that insight that I went to my *Random House Dictionary of the English Language, College Edition* from my college days, and began looking up each word to get the full impact. Here's the insight:

Get is a verb, used in this case as a command to ignite the personality aspect, "to acquire a mental grasp or command of its wholeness." *Ye* is a pronoun, "used objectively in second person singular." *Understanding* is a noun, used here to describe "the mental process of a person who comprehends; personal interpretation," ability to consciously grasp and retain knowledge on a subject, etc. *A* is used before a noun expressing quantity... in this case "one." *Soul's* is a possessive noun, the subject or doer of this task, the eternal life force and principle of this journey. *Point* is a noun that describes a specific location in a time space quadrant that can be used for orientation purposes. *Of* is a preposition, used to indicate the objective relation. *View* is a noun, used here to describe a process taking place within the mental, as well as visual perspective. *Of a* is a prepositional phrase, used here to draw awareness to the current doer. *Modern* is an adjective, used here to describe a current time sequence in a cycle of time. *Mystic,* is a noun, used to describe a person initiated into a specific process for the development of consciousness, which leads to the attainment of insight into what limited mental cognition defines as mystery, through transcending into wholeness. *Journey* is a noun, used here to describe a "passage, or progress from one stage to another."

Translation: *I, the Soul, command you George, the personality, to acquire a mental grasp of your wholeness in this now time. I, the Soul, ignite within you George, the personality, the mental process to comprehend and interpret this passage. I, the Soul, the eternal life force and principle of this passage, will describe to you from a specific location in a time space quadrant that will be used for orientation purposes, the objective relation of the process taking place within the mental, as well as visual perspective of what I, the Soul, am undertaking in this current time sequence as an initiate into the process for the development of consciousness through transcending the mysteries of the experiences into wholeness.*

Soul's growth: another perspective

As I thought and reflected on my understanding about the decoded message, another perspective of the message came up for me to consider. This perspective was that in this incarnation, my Soul had chosen to learn from the path of mysticism, the path of spiritual intuition of truths that transcend ordinary understanding, as opposed to learning from knowledge – the path of the head, or service – the path of the heart. And while I reflected on this mental understanding I heard my Soul's voice say, *"Unity is sensed in the heart: its intelligent application to life has to be worked out through knowledge. Balance is heart and head working together. Now, We, infinite I, and personality I, as a unit get to put the pieces together to see and comprehend the whole."*

This second perspective about the Soul enabled me to let go of my human level concept that the Soul knows it all. It's finito! My analysis of the decoded message suggested to me that there are ways and opportunities available to a Soul to grow in its evolution of understanding God. The decoded message had revealed and confirmed an ancient universal truth: Every aspect of creation, in some form or fashion, is evolving toward understanding the source of creation: GOD.

Amazing! I am truly amazed each day, as my mind stretches with this concept of *learning about God, and how God functions,* to discover how clever, wise and humorous God is. It's awesome! Totally awesome!

Decoding the title, learning about my Soul path, what this book is for me, and how it is to function in my life were just a few of the many lessons that I received while *writing* this book. The effect of these lessons jolted me out of self-doubting ego to one of excitement to learn and to be alive. And, what you have before you is seven years of George, the personality, peeling away layers upon layers of *him-self,* through writing, to figure out how to fulfill his Soul's request to tell the story of his journey home.

The Journey

All journeys, whether they're formal or informal, follow the Universal Law of Cycles, beginning, middle and end. I am very clear there are many journeys on the planet. Whose is the most difficult doesn't matter. What matters is that we awake, remember and own our Divine connection to the Source of All Life.

What is this book about?

Peeling the Onion is a collection of original poems that echo out into the world my experience of the various phases of my spiritual journey, from birth to the current time. My poems reveal the five unfolding phases of the life force, which is referred to in the Eastern Indian tradition as Kundalini and in the Oriental tradition as Chi.

The first phase of the journey is our descent from heaven, when we lose our awareness of our Divine connection. I call this phase Awakened to Sleep. Here I reflect on my early life experiences that deflected my awareness of my Divinity.

Once we fall asleep to our Divinity, we begin to live in the collective unconscious. I call this phase Living Dead. Here my poems reflect how the effects of falling asleep shaped and influenced how I lived and reacted to living in the collective unconscious phase of my life's journey.

Sleep, be it physical or mental, can only last for so long before there is a natural stirring to wake up. This stirring in the Eastern tradition is the life force beginning to wake up. Its western psychological equivalent is akin to the process of individuation. I call this phase Whispered Awake. In Whispered Awake I reflect on how I was guided back to opening up to my Soul's direction in my life.

Now that we are awake with the sense that there is more to ourselves, we begin the searching aspect of our journey to reconnect back to our divinity. I call this phase Exploring and Healing Myself. Here I reflect on the insights that came from my healing process.

When we've gone through searching, healing and have successfully reestablished our connection to our Divinity, we have come full circle. In the western transpersonal psychological model, this experience is referred to as ascension back into the Source. I call this phase of the journey Soul Revival. My final reflection on this ascension process has two aspects. The first aspect is about my early journey's ending. The second is a about a new phase of my journey, one that we all work hard to achieve.

If you are a friend, client or someone I've never met, as you turn the next page, from my heart to yours I dedicate the opening poem, "The Book," to you.

OPENING

THE BOOK

It started with the eyes
and ended with
a book.

Words alone mean nothing,
a single pebble in an empty room,
but combined cause my mind
to relax,
stretch,
like a slow moving river in deep thought.

It started with
your soft shy southern drawl
"How do I..."
and ended with
a book exploding my focus of my world—

a book so powerful that
I
  stop
      to
          reflect
                on
where I've been
what I felt
what I feel
where am
I
  going
    what
        am
        I
            Doing?

It started with a book
ended with a new vision
of life.

AWAKENED TO SLEEP

FIGHTING SLEEP

Seven pounds, six ounces
of pure light
knowing
only God.

Thirty pounds
of human flesh
getting hazy
knowing God.

Child! Don't talk
of Angels,
of God
Your reality is not real.
Thou shall be seen and not heard.
Go

to

sleep!

STOLEN CHILDHOOD

An innocent seven and a half year old
played hide and seek.

Ripped from my hiding place.
Assaulted sexually in the darkness.
Pain severed my childhood innocence. Shocked and
Emasculated forever in my mind.

I returned to my world
a wounded boy,
destined to become
a wounded man.

SALT IN THE WOUND

I witnessed him having sex with my sister.
  No! Stop! His eyes filled with raging fire he pressed his
    Cold knife against my ribs in anger,
        he whispered in my ear: "Fuck her!"
      Enraged at this monster, my uncle
        Scared I
        Take leave of my body and mind to save my sister.

SEVEN AND EIGHT

Seven and Eight
could have waited
because bliss was in full swing,
eating freshly picked potatoes from my grandmother's farm
red and black stained faces from eating wild blackberries.

Seven and Eight
didn't wait.
It thrust me into the world of
coarseness
roughness
harshness.
Crazed adults stabbing each other.
Sexual orgies in the basement.
All the things a child should not know.

Seven and Eight
taught me to hate–
a black storm cloud
blocking the Sun's vibrant light
shining on my ugly world
to mistrust
the thrust of this new life.

Seven and Eight
taught me
how far away I was
from laughing,
running naked under the water hose
on a hot summer day.

ESCAPEE AT TEN

Her rage,
was a bucking bull
with his balls tied tight,
could kill you
for violation of some unknown rule
or
just her plain madness.

Bound and whipped senseless
like a slave,
I escaped
The Home Insane Asylum
never to return.

NUMBING

At fifteen
my first funeral.
In the center below the pulpit,
stretched out in a child's white coffin
lay my eleven-year-old uncle.
I knew he was leaving,
but
I couldn't talk about it.

Grandma,
strong as an ox
weak as a lamb,
called out to her dead baby.
I knew she'd be leaving soon,
but
I couldn't talk about it.

June came.
She left.
I reached out my hand,
pulled down the Black Shade
of unawareness of God's other worlds.

Finally,
I'm
another
numb
human.

STRESS

Storing up the voices of failure,
    I take off my wings of creativity.
Tried placing my feet into the footprints
    of the path of the conformist.
Realized the system is a hungry whale yawning.
    It swallows you whole.
Ego gets destroyed.
Survival behavior sets in.
Screaming out, lashing
    out is how I shake hands with life.

A quiet voice inside me remembers,
whispers...

We
    are
        not
            meant
                to
                    fail!

LIVING DEAD

RIP IN MY SHADE

I sit in English class
lost in deep black space,
as my seventeen-year old mind
destroys my future of numbness.
I'm a comet crashing into
my old world of abuse, pain, and queerness.

From a place I long to forget,
my eyes open in a dream.
I can't stop
the odd questions,
strange arranged words
that flow from mind to paper.

I am a man in a straight jacket,
as I screamed at my demons:
"This isn't me!"
I hide my page of deviance
at the back of my notebook.

Now, there's a hole
in my black shade.

NIGHT'S A SLOW JOURNEY

One pulsing star
to guide me
a million strobe lights flashing
to confuse me
a world
so dark.

Night is
moving only
as
fast
as
I
crawl!

Night's a
slow
slow
s l o o o o w
journey.

MAGICIAN

He thrusts a blue mirror into my hands,
spins my chair.
My back faces the big wall mirror.
Looking into my hand mirror,
infinite images of the back of my head
emerge as big blossomed Sunflowers
in a straight line.

Real

is

Unreal.

I'm a magician's assistant.
My head's inside a black tube in a box.
He lifts the top of the tube,
but no head appears.

True

is

Untrue.

What is reality?

A crack
in the cosmic egg.
I look inside.

CERTAINLY UNCERTAIN

In the temple of Delphi,
I'm an Oracle
inside the vision
in the sacred water.

I'm a thread in a six inch thick black veil
of where and why
we settle were we do.
I speak truth.
You are confused.

Like lightning I cut through thick
billowy smoky gray veils of
how and why
we do the things we do.

My words
jolt you to life.

Hovering in a circle above the earth
we think we are angels.

But

are

we?

IN BETWEEN

In between my
heartaches,
tears,
loneliness,
pain,
sorrow,
sometimes I smile with joy.
I think of the people I've held
in my heart
and cry.

REBELLION

They told me, "Today is the first day of the rest of your life,"
yet I feel old and tired.

They told me, "Be kind, be gentle, be understanding,"
yet I feel hostile and mean.

They told me, "Be consistent, be flexible,"
yet I feel unpredictable, inflexible.

They told me, "Control me and be me,"
yet I feel like a tsunami rolling towards the beach.

They told me, "Give a smile to someone who frowns."
I gave and got back the frown.

They told me, "Be compassionate, be loving,"
yet I feel like delivering you to death in a tornado of fire.

They told me zillions of things to be,
but this morning I press one thousand pounds from my chest,
sweet like hot chocolate on a cold day,
gentle as a sleeping newborn.
Today I told them,
I'm gonna be me,
with me,
and for me.

VALIDATION

Nineteen.
Five feet, ten inches.
Dancer's hard body.
Outwardly,
wild as a black stallion.
Inwardly,
shy as a wild puppy.
I'm a magician
playing with your mind,
a tempter
playing with your body.
I smile for the camera,
bow for the crowd,
waiting to be cloaked
by your white roses
of Love.

PEELING THE ONION

The Sun's gentle rays
like a peacock feather
tickle my face.
I give birth –
laughter is my being.

Raindrops cover my face,
steal my laughter.
I become sadness.

Naked on the floor
beneath my window,
kissed all over
by the hot Sun,
I roar like a lion.

Portland's December icy rain on my bare head
turns me into a lonely sabertooth tiger
in a block of ice.

Hot jasmine body oil
melts my icy loneliness,
my long fingers intertwined
in your soft blond pubic hair.

The Phoenix of Loneliness
rises from the ashes of love,
flies into my chest.

Its beak of sorrow creates a whirlpool
of meaningless words in my head,
but the steady reverberation of the music
of my heartbeat makes me solid.

I am full inside myself,
centered like the Sun.

Deep in contemplation
like an ancient redwood tree rooted in the earth
I stand alone
against the hurricane winds of life.

In a charred landscape
I have survived life's earthquakes.
My strength is a jagged mountain range.

Exhausted from scaling the mountain of life,
so many times,
I sit on the boulder of understanding.
Absorbed into its sweet warm comfort,
I give birth to closeness and love.

I am a wandering sadhu in love.
Staring into the Ganges I find myself searching for
the shifting ray of knowledge
that confuses my certainty.

Tumbling across the Universe
in a crystal ball of confusion,
I steal the golden ring.
Clutching it to my hardened heart,
a question, with its skilled surgeon's hands, opens me.

In the question I find myself again.

IF

If only tears would pour from my eyes,
I might be able to see more clearly.
If the tears would come,
I could wipe the confusion from my soul.
If only the tears could come,
with a new smile I could begin
to put together puzzle pieces of me.
If only the tears could come,
I could...

but I can't.

OUT OF TOUCH

Hanging
on a New York gallery wall
me
a black and white nude photo
shot from the back.
I was reaching for the light
shining down from heaven.

Alone, shy,
hiding in the shadows
from the New York glitterati,
hungry birds of prey
demanding to feast on my flesh.

At last I
find myself
within
the
inner circle.

Out of touch
from all who
appear
real.

Out of touch
from the soft lights,

all the clouds of
smoke
that fill the
air.
Out of touch
yes
Out of touch
because
I've been in touch
In touch
In touch
with out of touch

and I found that
touched by the hand of God,
out of touch
will one day
be
in Touch.

SUMMER OF '79

Here's to you, last summer of the seventies!
Filled with dreams dancing with Isis
in the moonlight by the Sphinx,
hopes of crushing sexist minds like hot burnt toast,
desires that overshadow the ecstasy
of a lover's skilled hands stroking the back of my neck,
illusions of strong sun brown hands reaching through
the pressing crowds to touch me,
heat emanating from my stomach like the desert sun.

Sweat, like fresh pressed wine, covers my skin,
laughter, like a bull elephant making love,
roars from my throat,
tears of anger from having my creative approach to living
outside the grey faceless box of life
being rejected,
hopes of sacred dance
being embraced by the banks of the Nile,
my fears of going insane,
and, Oh God, least I forget
Reality?

I know now that time is
and always will be,
Oroborus, the snake without end.
I say amen to the Creator in all of us.

Upon the altar of life,
I gracefully offer up my youth
in exchange for
sanity and wisdom.

Ah yes,
My memories of the summer of 1979 –
crying in a New York City phone booth
asking a friend for shelter,
begging in Casa Blanca
to stay and dance the sun into the sky,
confused by my emotions in Cairo,
looking for a street of gold.
I found a street of broken dreams and promises.

FADE TO NOTHING

Fourteen years of being

a couple.

Fourteen days of being

single.

Broken hearted, I stand

before a high tech microphone,

poised

to record my artistic

highs and lows

like a dying man

breathing out his last breath.

I am a faded voice echoing in a canyon

as I hold the last note

and

fade

into

nothingness.

ROCK IN WATER

When I first saw you
I was stunned.
I had seen your picture before—
big, brown, burly weather-shaped
bulky mass
surrounded by water,
seducing me to come closer.

I waded
through the icy
Pacific Ocean,
climbed upon your strong
hard body.
Like a vine wrapped around a Banyan tree,
we embraced,
and as I loved you,
the maddening loneliness for home
eating at my raw storm-tossed heart
fell into the icy water.

Your embrace gave me back
my connection
to the Earth.

A fourteen-year game of push-pull love
was crushed in seconds.

Sad,
angry,
exhausted,
I fell asleep with tears of relief
flowing from my eyes.

You softly entered into my lonely
heart
as if I were a waiting warm bed
of flannel sheets on a cold winter night.

I climbed upon your tender
hard body,
I sang your secret mantra out loud
like a Rock in the Water.

Exhausted from churning the ocean
with our undulating wave of love
as I gently laid upon you,
the silent teacher of teachers.
You embraced me again,
showing me how to survive
this world of deception.

WHISPERED AWAKE

WHISPERING

From a bow shaped mouth,
a breathy voice
warms my cold listening ear.

Words, like crashing cymbals, reverberate,
through the waters of my brain,
creating emotional whirlpools of
laughter and delight,
sexual passion from secret love notes
slipped into my pants pocket.
Fantasies of heroic acts of bravado
flow like a rushing river through my body.

Whispered sacred words enter my ear,
sweet music of a flute
riding on a summer night's breeze

    to

        awaken

           infinity.

NO RETURN

In a deep sleep for three days,
my first conscious meeting
with my Soul,
my life changed
forever.

Nineteen years old, Earth time,
in a silver room with three steps,
wrapped in luminescent light
where my Soul and Guardian stood
loving me inside a small golden orb of light.

I hated living,
my heart cold and dead,
killed by
twisted adults and children that caused pain
to my young tender body.
I was suffering from fear of the next violation,
sorrow from the weariness of having to fight for my life,
suffering from loneliness
in the steel fortress I built in order to survive.
"I want out!" I screamed.

I'm a dying man
in need of love
clinging to his life.
I pleaded

I begged
for my eternal freedom.

"Incomplete."
"No return,"
You said.

Wanting You I surrendered
like a dew drop on a dry leaf
absorbed back into the surging river of
life.

SPIRITUAL MUSE

You glowed like Venus in the evening sky.
I called out your name in the dark doorway,
surrounded by silver light.

My spiritual muse appeared
as a California surfer girl,
blue eyes like the ocean sky
smile hotter than the Sun's equator,
as you entered my heart.

Half awake,
distant and suspicious of people,
frustrated
with my life
I heard you whisper your magical incantation
into my right ear.
You awakened my heart,
tore another veil from my eyes.

You held me in your arms,
like a mother cat carrying her kitten
in her mouth
and carried me to the golden
light filled doorway.
Wearing a loincloth and my begging bowl I stepped through
sat down under the light filled dome
in a sinking temple in the Ganges in the City of the Dead
to begin my Eastern journey.

GLADYS

With a wounded heart
I walked into your yellow kitchen.
You sat at the corner of the table
with silent tears
rolling down your cheeks.
You were a teacher, the daughter of Jewish immigrants.

I was the young black boy who
cut your grass
and cleaned your house.
I painted your yellow kitchen
and asked, "Why are you crying?"

Your silence became sobs.
You told me the child who threw a book in your class
was crying for help.
You cared about him
and spoke to the principal about his pain.
No one listened.
The system tossed the child aside,
and your heart hurt.

As the sun set over the Hudson River,
I walked out of your yellow kitchen
with my heart filled
with hope
with love.
I now strive for success,
knowing you saw my innocent pain.
My life has been transformed by your
tears of love.

CHANGED MY MIND

Emotionally exhausted
with an aching heart
from knowing I've grown
beyond your style of human love,
alone
with silent tears flowing softly
down my velvet brown cheeks,
I fell asleep
in a misty haze on my futon.

Watching my old life flow
through my closed eyes,
I heard your strong soft voice,
"You belong to me!"

"I'm not ready yet," I cried.

"If I must wait
until you become a widower,
then I will!"

Like a drill bit that broke through
to underground rushing water,
my tears
like a stream
rushed down my sleeping face.

I watched you
through my closed eyes
as your slender arms reached out and held me firmly.
Your smooth fingers tenderly slid down
the deep muscle groove in my back.
Your gentle kiss on my tear filled eyes
comforted me.

I love you.
I belong to you.
Come,
I'm ready now.

EXPLORING AND HEALING MYSELF

COSMIC TENNIS

Announcer: We're on the Cosmic Tennis Court of Evolution.
Our players are Universal Self versus small self.

The grand prize: Unity Consciousness and Life in Bliss.

The ball is composed of Ego.
Small self is about to serve.
He wants to remain small,
so he's going to play rough.

small
self: "Okay, I'll run him all over the universe.
He'll get so tired and give up the quest for unity.
I'm going to remain me."

Universal
Self: "Poor boy—doesn't he realize we're one?
Doesn't he know that life is evolutionary,
growth toward what I want to give him...
Unity."

small
self: "I have to stay alert to his gentleness.
I'll hit Ego with a hard slam
to the back court."

Universal
Self: "Nice Shot. Let me be gentle with him.
I'll give him a ball with a love spin
right at his feet."

LIFE IS AN ACRONYM

Look

Inside

For

Enlightenment

WHEEL OF LIFE

Another Time
Another Face
Another Love
Another Place

The ancient wheel of life
turned in its orbit within snake eyed slits,
swims into my life

in a river of boiling water.

KEEPER OF THE GATES

My mind explodes like a house hit by an atom bomb.
The king cobra slithers underneath the gate
of the darkest cave of my mind,
piercing my illusion of openness
with its lightning bite of truth.

I pry open the closed gates
to find another facet of my small self
and grapple with the ugly of uglies
that causes me to function in a self destructive way.

Gotta keep the door open!
Have to let the light shine way in there
to remove my darkness.

EGO BUSTING

My ego,
bigger than life,
fits on the head of a pin.

With outstretched arms I radiate
healing to the world.

Beloved One,
in the world of pain and suffering,
your offering is a tiny spark,
your words, an atom
silenced by the noise of life.

Beloved One,
your actions, bigger than life,
fit on the head of a pin.

Your love, like you,
an infinitesimal grain of sand,
fits on the head of a pin
with a million angels
dancing and singing God's praise.

WAITING FOR PERFECTION

Like a seasoned actor with
memorized lines,
I am a wild belly dancer with
controlled rehearsed moves.
With confidence and self-control
of my perfection,
I walk with my ego
across life's stage of improvisation
and fall down.

Waiting for perfection
is just another dance
in the ego's resistance.

TRUTH BLOCKS

Rigid to growth.
Egotistical to cover the fear.
Skeptical towards truth.
Insensitive to life.
Stubborn in beliefs, like clinging ivy rooted to old emotions.
Tyrannical in behavior.
Arrogant towards God.
Numb to the Soul's Love.
Critical of creation for not conforming to my desires.
Evasive to commitment.

Welcome to **RESISTANCE**.

SPLIT SECOND

One micron is all I have
to perform
the task:
Emotions or heart?
Destruction or creation?
Peace or turmoil?
Acceptance or rejection?
Love or not love?
Conditional love or unconditional Love?
Stay or go?
Laugh or weep?
Heal or wound?
Trust or mistrust?
Sex or celibacy?
Christ or Judas?

FEELING GOD

I thought God was a white,
angry,
vengeful
man in the center of the Milky Way
sitting on a golden throne.

I AM not!
That illusion is your distorted thinking.

When a newborn nuzzles its tiny innocent
face into my neck,
my heart, like an oil vein pierced by a drill,
explodes with unconditional love.
I'm saturated to my core
in gratitude for the creator of all life.

That is Truth. I AM Love.
I live deep in your Heart.

To know God
I take my mind like a marshmallow on a twig,
thrust it into the blazing fire of feelings.
Mind's charred crusty outer shell of beliefs
crumbles as I bite down
and the soft inside of innocence slowly slides down my
throat.

I
feel
you
inside,
and you know me.

OPENING THE WINDOW

You said, "I am like a window.
I let Light in and show you the infinite sky."

My window is locked and covered
by a black shade.

When I lift up the black shade
and look down I see people,
like chickens stuffed into crowded cages,
fighting to survive.
When I look up
beyond the rooftops of misery
into the sky,
the fingertips of infinity
motion to me, chant, "Come here!"

I've seen one millionth
of the infinite vastness
and want more.

Today I agreed to open the window
and let the air purify me.
I inhale life's electricity and grow wings.

Recharged, I poked my head outside the window
looked up and saw more infinity–
the North Star above me,
Pleiades to my left.

I am not afraid.

The fingers of infinity motion: "Come!"
I exhale limitation from my lungs,
reach out my hand,
touching infinity's velvety fingertips
and leap into the open sky.

LOVE'S DREAM

Exhausted from weeping
over the eons of ignorance and distance
you, the asleep ones,
have wedged between us,
my heart fell asleep.

Mother God
silently floated into her sleeping child's room
and placed her butterfly kiss
upon my leaden heart.
Like a cactus revived by desert rain,
I was inspired to live again.

Turned on by love's kiss,
my heart said,
Get up!
I was a rooster
crowing *I love you* to the world
at the Sun's first ray.

Freed from the illusion of separation,
filled, ready to explode,
I awakened
like a gale wind set free.

PURIFICATION

A flowing muddy river of old memories
lights up my mind.
Its swollen waves of emotions
destroy my banks of peace,
but it's only purification going on.

As icy cold waters
of purification wash over me,
painful memories of abuse chill me to the bone.
My body flinches as the pain dissolves.

Now I am filled with memories
of pressing my five year old handprints
in fresh dough to give to Grandpa Alvin for dinner.
I am combing Grandma Sara's thick long black hair
while she churned the ice cream maker
after Sunday's church.
The icy water warms with joy
and begins to soften my cold heart.
It's only purification going on.

Cold,
    warm,
        muddy
            waves of memories
light up my mind.
I become aware
of how far away I am
from being pure.

MY PARENTS-MYSELF

In the river of my emotions, I take my pan of psyche,
reach down and scoop up the black
silt from the bottom.
Gently swirling my pan of psyche in the water,
a miner panning for gold,
I find a thought shard —
my parents' inability to heal their wounds
and battle weary abusive childhoods.
Another swirl and a stone called
I believed I'm destined to live your lives
by my words and actions
 is uncovered.

Jolted to reality, I wade
to the rock of reflection
rising high above the water.
Sitting with eyes wide open,
I look into my pan.
I've come to discover
that which I thought about you,
believed you to be —
my parents —
is myself.

FATHER

To the invisible father
who walked into my turbulent life and
disappeared into thin air,
whom I caught
only a fleeting glimpse of
in my life,
I know you
better than if I saw you.

HAVE TO GIVE IT UP

Oh God! Here I am desolate
in frigid subzero Fairfield Iowa.
Memories of too many beatings
and relationships fights
are running through
my mind,
causing the pain of my
childhood
to hurt again.
Have to give it up.

I'm older now,
but the pain
is just as raw
as it was the first time.
Have to give it up.

All the years
I nurtured these hurts
like a mushroom growing on a decaying tree
only to become blind
to their pain.
Have to give it up.

I was a helpless eight-year-old
listening in the night
to your screams of pain
as you were being beaten
in the bathroom by your boyfriend.
Now I'm a helpless thirty-four-year-old
sitting in deep meditation

listening to the echos in my heart,
only now I see how your feelings
of unworthiness and anger
shaped my life.
It tore us apart
and kept us apart.
You, not knowing
how I felt inside
helpless to help you find your dignity
and let go of your rage against black men,
unable to explain
my inner feelings of fear and powerlessness to protect you,
and you with your lost dignity
helpless to hide your hurt,
anger and frustrations.
Have to give it up.

We're still apart
you still not knowing
how
I feel inside,
praying that you find your dignity and gentleness,
and me working to heal
the wounded hearts of childhood.

You've turned toward religion.
I've turned inward,
and we both see yesterday
for what it was,
God's healing grace for what it will be.
Don't have to give this up.

APOLOGY

To all of you who have attempted
to open my heart to love
and whom I hurt in the process,

I apologize.

I was engulfed in a hurt
so powerful and overpowering,
I wore black eye patches
that blinded me to the tenderness of love
and life all around me.

You've tried to reach me
with your gentle hugs
and tender kisses
to soothe my wounded heart.
Lord knows, you've tried,
but I hurt you with my steel walls
and cold icy stares
as you cried for my love.
Now all I can do is

apologize

for my ignorance of the past
as I pushed you away
like a rebellious two-year old
and to ask for your forgiveness
and blessings.

As I become more enlightened
with each passing day,
all I do when I think of you is

apologize.

THREE SIMPLE WORDS

In all the universe there are
no more powerful words than...

Three simple yet complex words
have the ability to
uplift, brighten,
and soften the stoneface
facade of all creatures in creation.

Three simple words
two pronouns and a noun
can do so much, yet they're used
so rarely in our insane rat race lives.

To speak these words from the head
a magician mumbling his incantation
to a dead rock.
To hear these words with the ears
is to catch only a faint
flicker of their essence.
To see these words with the eyes
is like speed reading a palm
by candlelight.

To experience the fullness
of all of creation and the universe,
you must experience life with the heart,
for the simple heart
in its innocence and quiet
unfolds all that is within us.

Three simple words —

I
    love
         you!

MEN'S INITIATION TALISMAN

Three inch blood red leather pouch
filled with sacred herbs and stones,
tied with a dark brown leather cord,
one carved white bead
as a tunnel to the other world.
Suspended from my neck in honor of
my sacred initiation into
Manhood,
your blood touches my heart.
With you my body and mind are like a
clear mountain lake.
Basking in the sun's warm soothing rays
I am Man!

I've danced the rhythmical steps of
Anger and Rage
Love and Hate
Passion and Cold
Fear and Joy
too long.

You have taken me to sacred brotherhood,
killed my fear of men.
I can never go back.
I am a man who has died to the old male ways of manhood.
I am reborn.

I am your Wildman,
King,
Warrior,
Priest,
Magician,
Lover.
I am Sacred Man!

ENLIGHTENED SEXUALITY

A room filled with golden light.

A bed with white silk sheets,
a blood red silk heart
shaped pillow.

I didn't see you,
but I felt your presence in the room.

A basket of woven red and yellow roses
with one bright red apple,
a purple cluster of fat juicy grapes
on the pillow.

Beside the basket, a parchment scroll
tied with a yellow ribbon of rubies and diamonds,
where I felt your essence waiting for me to untie.

Savoring your anticipation
like a drop of honey suspended from a spoon
waiting to fall,
I slowly untied and unrolled the parchment.
My body tingled with
anticipation
as I read your words:
The red apple is for Knowledge.
The cluster of deep purple grapes is for sensuous pleasure.

Choose wisely, for I will make love to you that way.

Not fair! No either/or! I want
And!
I screamed.
I sat on the bed, took the yellow
ribbon of rubies and diamonds,
tied it around my cock and balls
like the scroll.

I picked up the apple,
took one deep purple grape
like a slice of cheese,
placed it on top
and ate it.

And!
I whispered
this is how you will love me.

I lay down on a bed of golden light.
Your essence of crushed opals and diamonds covered me.
And!
this is how you loved me.

LIT UP

Encased in a shimmering ball
of golden brown flesh,
I entered the world
lit up by God's Light.

Shadows
like horny men
burning with passion's fire
cannot dim my light.

Surrounded by
the woes of the world
jealousy, hate and anger
I burn holes through them
like a canvas lampshade.

Like a searchlight
shining into a starless midnight sky,
I make love

24/7
365
non stop
lit by God's light.

COAL TO DIAMOND

Living from a heart surrounded by
thick ice glacier walls
my speech appeared to be
very rude.

The scabs of lack of self-love,
covered my wounded heart.
I lunged at life
like crude oil shooting from the Earth.

I'm a lewd lump of coal chiseled by
humanity's cruel and thoughtless behavior
tossed into the hands of the diamond cutter.

Going through refinement, my
melted glaciers have merged into the quiet ocean,
scabbed heart smoothed by God's love.

All that is left now
is
a polished jewel.

SLOW COOKER ON A HIGH FLAME

Slow cooker on a high flame
inside my head and heart.
The silly questions,
raunchy thoughts,
questions of is this—or anything
for that matter—Real?

Sometimes in my heart I know this,
as the slow cooker on a high flame
burns my sense of certainty.
Am I love?
Does Guru care?
Do I care?
Am I deluding myself
with a false sense of understanding?

Instructions: Take one confused, hurt, angry human.
Insert the rod of transcendence.
Hang over a high flame of Love of God
and slowly turn until all the fat
of ignorance is melted,
leaving the tenderness of Being exposed.

Remove from the flame and cool
with the Breath of Bliss.
Marinate in the nectar of Joy.
After some time cook again
very slowly on a high flame of Love.

THE WAIT

Valentine's Day.
The volcano has erupted.

Emotional hurricane
is gathering more energy.

I rage like a tornado,
screaming with the force of a gale wind.

Storm his door.
Wring his neck.
Sit and wait.

He leaves
and I'm forced to
sit and wait.

I hate this tactic!
I loath the energy it brings.

Is the Guru a wise man
or a skilled manipulator?

I sit.
I rage.
I wait.
I scream.

Calmness
is trying to overtake me,
but I fight its force.
Nothing much to do except
sit and wait.

CALL OF THE MASTER

Through the uproar
of my emotional storm,
I saw you inside the Sun.
You said, "Come to Me."

I tried to come
but
I
hurt inside.

You smiled through the Sun's aura,
reached out and said,
"Come to Me."

I gave you my hand
and
Peace
d
e
s
c
e
n
d
e
d.

BURSTING THE BUBBLE

When you think you've mastered it all—
the imp of conformity,
        the mischievous sprite of isolation,
            demons of self-hatred—
there in your shadow
      like a cobra with its spread hood:
        waiting to strike
          you find your darkest
emotion blocking your light.

This one is a little bigger than the others
and twice as strong.

You know what's going on,
yet there's nothing to do except wait.

I heard the Master's song
falling on my heart.
Each word, each magnificent note, absorbed
like a balloon in need of air,
caused my shrunken heart of love to grow again.
Suddenly my bubble burst,
leaving me so full I overflowed.

The fear, the doubt, the negativity
dissolved like sandalwood incense
burned on an altar by a river.

Now my heart is filled
with love and silence.

My heart heard the Master's song
of gratitude to God.
His notes became the fibers of my body,
infusing the space between my cells with gratitude.
His silence infused my silence
like the sun filling the sky with light.
His words steeped into my heart
like herbs soaked in hot water,
causing my bubble to burst.

IN LOVE

In the ocean of your Love,
I was conceived.

In the ocean of your Love,
I was born.

In the silence of your presence,
I become alive
like the first kiss of true love,
while my ego fights for its illusion.

In the presence of your Love
I become the sun, the moon, and the stars.
And even in my ego's fight and flight,
like a trapped wild lion
I still feel your Love.

In the presence of your Presence,
a ray of full moonlight disappearing into the sun,
I surrender all that
I Am
was
and will become.

PERSONAL POWER

Personal Power is
Being
connected to
the true source of
Creation
and
doing what you
know to be
in harmony with
the Laws of the Universe
for any given moment in time and space.

Personal Power is
Being
God's fully developed,
conscious
Radiant Light.

SEE – SAW

Sometimes I feel like I'm on a see-saw,
up and down so quickly.

When I see the people of this world,
fireflies in a dark dense forest,
flickering lights,
walking in and out of other worlds
inside an expanding universe,
I'm thrilled at how we love and laugh like children
at play in the celestial sandbox.

When I see the dragon
of the fear of change
breathe its fire of resistance
into the unlocked eyes of man,
I'm saddened at how we convert

our love and laughter
into hate and death.

With perfect balance and poise,
I stand on the fulcrum point of the see-saw,
like a juggler balancing the solar system
while standing on the head of a pin.
I balance my day-to-day life
while standing of the ball of joy.

Never minding the See

Never minding the Saw

Enjoying the Transcendental State
of tranquil evenness
                    resting in the arms of my beloved,
                                    on the way home.

DECISION

Amidst swirling winds of emotions,
I control the winds.

In the middle of
crashing waves of thoughts,
I Am silence.

Surrounded by an army of love and wonder,
I am calm—
for this is who I truly am.

It's amazing how a decision,
in
one
split
second,
ruled by emotions,
can either
destroy
or
create.

A decision
from the Heart of Silence
can only bring
PEACE.

INTEGRATED AWARENESS

Her heavenly tones took me
beyond my narrow psychic belief
of being a womb
for unseen spirits to visit this world.

I exhaled the crowded
subway chatter of my mind
and entered into the universe of
no-mind.

Within me,
my Soul
spoke through me.

I am now
a universal waiter for God.

RECEIVING

Receiving
is fully accepting the truth
that all things come
from God
and that we
are not
the sole source
of our supply.

Receiving is being humble
yet gracious
to our benefactor.

Receiving is owning
every flawed diamond facet
of your personality.

Receiving is being
open
at all times
to our source
and being
thankful
for
the ability to smell and taste
the flavors of life
as you walk among its stalls,
being able to feel the textures of emotions—
like grades of spun silk rubbed against your body,
the in-breath that gives you life.

LEATHER VELVET GLOVES

Long golden honey
graceful fingers.
Strong masculine veins
protrude under the skin
like mountain ranges,
velvety to touch.

Soft, strong fingers
delicately glide across your skin
like butterflies
floating on an invisible
summer breeze,
enticing you to kiss their strength.

Touch liquifies your mind
as you fall asleep to
its powerful grip of restraint.

Ageless wisdom
etched in the palms
conceals secrets
available only to an inquiring
body and mind.

Come.
Take my hand.

NEW LIFE

I sit cross-legged
on a smooth flat rock
above a stream,
our life force pulsing as one.
Like a yogi in the Absolute,
my mind is reflective.

Red,
yellow,
burnt orange leaves
like whispering clouds with changing faces
quietly stir on a windless day
and float past my watchful eyes...

my anger and disappointment,
life's unfulfilled dreams and broken promises,

old wisdom I called upon
to survive on my journey,

the passion I used
to move through my tumultuous life.

Tears fall from my eyes
like rough hewn stones
thrown into a Zen pond,

creating
    soft
      distinct
        concentric
          rings of life
            in the water.

I'm ready to begin a new life.

SOUL REVIVAL

OPENING OF THE GATES

The gates are beginning to open.

I feel the ancient hand of wisdom
reach through the silver cosmic curtain
to grab my doorknob heart.
I long to feel its firm gentle grip,
yet I'm afraid I'll implode like the Sun's hot gases.
Today, I feel the tip of God's
love arrow.
Tomorrow, like a hammer hitting glass,
it will smash open my gate of ignorance.

As I peek through those gossamer golden gates,
I see what I lost,
my front row seat at Mother-Father God's feet.
I long to sit and revel in their crystalline love,
but am I ready
to dissolve my ego
and become a human beacon of Divine Light?

Today, only the bud of yearning.
Tomorrow, the flower of full knowledge,
the opening of the gates.

IT DOESN'T MATTER

It doesn't matter
about
race,
creed,
social status,
sex,
or
sexual preference.

It doesn't matter
if you
have a path
or
are pathless.

All that matters to God
is that
you get lit
with His fire,
His passion,
His Love.

TRAITS OF GOD

Humility,
> not Ego.

Wisdom,
> not an intellect stuffed with book learning.

Self-assuredness,
> not cockiness.

Compassion,
> not an ice-cube heart.

Loving,
> not solitary confinement.

Caring,
> not turning your eyes away from the abuse,
> that staggers in front of you.
> Or covering your ears to keep from hearing the
>> cries for help
> that shatter your dream of peace and safety.

All inclusive,
> not living in a monochrome world.

Open minded,
> not a mind sealed in a time capsule
> buried in a mountain.

Patience,
> not rushing to tackle life.

Silence,
> not a head stuffed and overflowing
> with meaningless sounds.

Purposefulness,
> not aimlessly drifting on a log
> in the sea of life.

Let God sow His traits deep
into your barren mind.
Let His love feed your fertile heart,
and your enlightenment will grow to feed creation.

CLEAR LIGHT

Today
I realized
that what I was looking for

in something
and some place

is in
No-thing,
and no place.

HOW LONG MY GOD? HOW LONG?

How long my God?
How long
before I can meet you
face to face?

I have opened the gates of my heart
where the river of love flows.
I have opened the window of my mind
to your omnipresent Self,
yet like an endless horizon on the silent ocean
you seem so far away,
even though I know You're here
inside
outside
beside me
around me like a pregnant woman.

How long my God?
How long
before my twisted wave-filled path
comes to rest at Your feet,
before my heart and mind
desire no other
but you
at all times?

I hunger day by day
as time crescendos inside my soul
to merge within
Your infinite Being.

I cry out in my soul,
How long?
My God!
How long?

MANSION

In my Father's house
there are as many rooms as the stars
beyond our galaxy,
and one of them is mine.
As I draw nearer to my Father's house,
my joy builds,
yet I am fearful of being struck
by His lightening bolt of Love.
Should I turn back?
Will I make it home?

I ran away from home one moonless night
two thousand years ago.
I know it made Him sad.
Even though I stole the horses of ego
and pain for my journey
and left his precious mansion,
which is filled with
Love,
Peace,
Harmony and
Joy,
I know my Father loves me.
He watches my labored footsteps
through His window of forgiveness.

In my Father's house, my Mother waits for me
with the sweet love only a mother can give.
My sisters and brothers unlink the family circle of woven arms
as I run to embrace them
so that we can fill the heavens
like rambunctious children with joy and love.

The road to my Father's house is getting shorter and shorter.
As I look up in the early morning light,
I see shimmering golden bricks.
My body shakes with delight,
and my mind trembles.
I know that no matter where I've been
or what I've thought before,
when I knock on the door
and my Father holds me in his arms,
my journey is over.
My Father told me
I'm always welcome home.

DEATH

Enmeshed in my web of ignorance and self-judgment,
a lamb with tied legs waiting to be slaughtered,
I cried out to be free,
to play among the galaxies with the angels.

Cloaked in an iridescent robe, my Soul said:

"Death, the transition, is more difficult
than death the physical.

Transition is life.

The grotesque gargoyle shadows
suddenly appearing on your blank wall,
shifting like clouds blowing across the sun's face
are reflections of a mind
unfocused on God.

You have chosen to become a polished
jewel in God's crown.
You have asked to live in the full light of His Love.
You have dedicated your frail human body
to grow,
live
and serve beyond the restrictions
of time, space and limited book filled intellect,
and thou shall receive in joy.
Enjoy!"

FROM 0 TO OVERFLOW

I used to have zero love
for others and even less
for myself,
but now I close my eyes
and overflow.

I am a seed slowly and steadily
sprouting in the earth's womb,
as I begin to realize
the joy of loving.
With the sun's nurturing light in my universe,
I have become a sweet passion fruit
ready to be plucked.

My life has skyrocketed
from zero to overflow.
With my eyes wide open
my mind is in full drive,
and my heart's on overflow.

INTENTION

It's not leaping from peak to peak
or creeping from one book of knowledge to the next.
It's intention.

It's not how you execute your jumps and crawls;
it's sincere desire.

It is not about the how to diagram
the ivory tower reasoning of why
or the way the demon ego was skillfully
tied up and gagged.

It's the intention.

The intention of being
for God,
and
God Alone.

EMPOWERMENT

I'm tired from wielding my sword of false power.
The choking hand of powerlessness
reaches into my desperate intellect
to grab my will to live.

For three-days I fast and vision quest.
I walk across hot coals,
wear power suits to broadcast
my authority,
a shadow hiding in full sunlight
slipping through my clutching fingers.

Like the Sun propelled
by the unseen hand of God

Empowerment
is
on
the Soul's
terms,
not
ours.

ELEMENTAL LIFE

As I stepped on the earth,
I realized the Earth in me.
As the Sun's rays awakened my face
I became conscious of the Sun/Son in me.

Caressed by the supple wind's gentle breath
I become the Air.
Sitting on a rough-hewn log in the woods,
my eyes like a microscope slowly gaze
across the clear lake
that is my face.

I feel the water flowing from within me.
I become the all-permeating ether of life.
I listen to the echo that moves
within the motionless space around me.
I am the sound of a newborn
and the silence of a star in the midnight sky.

SURRENDER

I stopped.

I listened.

I obeyed the Silence.

Om shanti.

ETERNITY

I welcome myself
inside
the inner circle
where I AM
and always will Be.

Encircled by all the races of the world,
I AM
and always will Be.

Entwined like two ropes in a knot,
physical love still makes me
realize I AM
and always will Be.

Whether I am the Blue Pearl
suspended in empty space
or
the Northern Lights dancing and weaving
my magic in the night sky
or even
a meteor shower falling to Earth,
I
AM
and
ALWAYS
WILL
Be.

SOUL IMPLANT

On August 4, 1998
after morning meditation,
in honor of surviving
fifty years of hard life,
I bowed down
and gave thanks to God
for HIS Grace in my life.

Hit in my back
like a potato farmer piercing the earth with a hoe
by a bolt of lightening,
my heart chakra burst open
and my Soul stepped in.

Calm and peaceful inside
I knelt,
sobbing like a thunderstorm
wailing like a coyote at the moon
at my death
and my rebirth
into a golden Being of Light.

SOUL EXPANSION

In hot Atlanta
on August 30, 1998
I sat in prayer
in a grand hotel conference room,
ceiling lights glowing like soft candle light
among four hundred and fifty people.
I felt every cell of my body
being filled
lovingly
gently
with the essence of my Soul.

I'm a marble statue
in silence
resting
across my bed,
tenderly whispered to life
by my Soul's soft sweet voice:
"I have waited for you to be ready for fifty years.
Now we can begin to do our work in the world."

A gentle river of silent tears rolled down my face
as I bathed in that precious moment,
filled like the ocean with serenity
and love
that came from the core
of my heart
and silence.

I wanted to
reach out
with my strong arms
and embrace the turbulent world,
it's a perpetual atomic clock's endless ticking.

SOUL SEALED

Like a yogi
I sit cross-legged
in the October woods
listening to words of
ancient wisdom.
Sacred sounds enter my ears
and dissolve into my being
like butter on hot bread from the oven.
Inside me, nothingness blossoms
like morning dew,
appearing like magic on fallen golden leaves and dry grass.

My life's a dry twig
snapped by a heavy foot.
My Soul sits in full lotus,
gazing out at the lake's horizon.
Earth
Wind
Fire
and
Ether
join hands and dance
into my quiet heart.

An old door
gently pushes closed
and seals itself with hot wax.
I hear the final
snap of my old life
like a kernel of popcorn
bursting from the heat.
Tears quietly flow
as I dissolve into nothingness.

GRATITUDE

Thank you God
for giving me
more than I can say.

I dedicate my essence
to you for eternity.

May I gracefully love others
as you so gracefully love.

Amen.

INVITATION

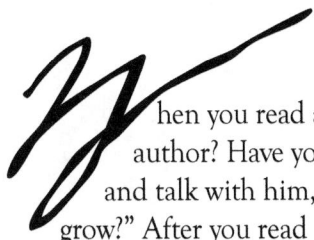

hen you read a book, have you ever wanted to meet the author? Have you ever thought, "If I could look into his eyes and talk with him, what else could I learn that would help me grow?" After you read a book that gives you another perspective to view your life and the world around you, what happens to your mind? Are you inspired? Is your creativity stimulated? Is your heart open? Are there points or questions that arise from deep inside you that you'd like to explore?

As the author of Peeling the Onion, I discovered a part of me that would enjoy the opportunity to look into your eyes, to hear you laugh or perhaps shed a tear or two. I found myself wanting to flow with you as a current inside the river of your life, to walk with you, talk about the poems, respond to your questions, and enjoy the stories that flowed freely in the air about our journeys.

If we had these thoughts and feelings prior to modern technology, the only choices available for book discussions and interaction would be with a small circle of friends, a book club, or a letter to the author. However, in today's modern world with technology and global communication networks, we have a range of communication possibilities, such as in-person lectures, video, teleconferencing, and workshops available to choose from.

Peeling the Onion invited you to expand and explore your world— an invitation you graciously accepted. I now expand the invitation by offering to read, sign and discuss the book at an event in your area. I can be contacted at www.georgejames.org so we can make it happen.

The prayer that I hold in my heart for you is that you open wider, deepen your connection to your Soul, and turn up the brightness of your inner light to light the world. I'm looking forward to meeting you soon.

Blessings,
George James